"He looked good, like sin in a suit."

KITCHEN
Lunch. Dinner. Brunch.
P 212.425.7171

P

EXCHANGE PLACE
BEAVER ST
STONE ST
HANOVER SQUARE
PEARL ST
WATER ST
PINE ST
CEDAR ST
LIBERTY ST
MAIDEN LANE
JOHN ST
FULTON ST
A C

light at
M & 1AM.

892
mbi
h
K

850

bank

CREATION

ALPIN

MICHAEL

3N10

REGAL

TD

ELMSLEY W

NEW YORK POST
FORWARD

Pay at
BOBBY

hion Optical
CHANGE G
CHAN

H&M

FLEX
SPENDING
DOLLARS

MEZZANINE 2nd FL
MAIN FLOOR CELLAR
AND SUBCELLAR

SYSCO

L & M TOURS

POL
RESPECT

ARENSON

Bank of Ameri

America

FUSO
FC-SP

MITSU

TITAN

L & M TOURS
86
& M TOURS

Onion Crunch
YUM, YUM, YUM!
HOT DOG

TOURS

P

.com
NOW
HIRING
M2035

again.
joy the Coke.
cycle the bottle.

CARRIER

T6429

3C24

7K41
NYC

ups

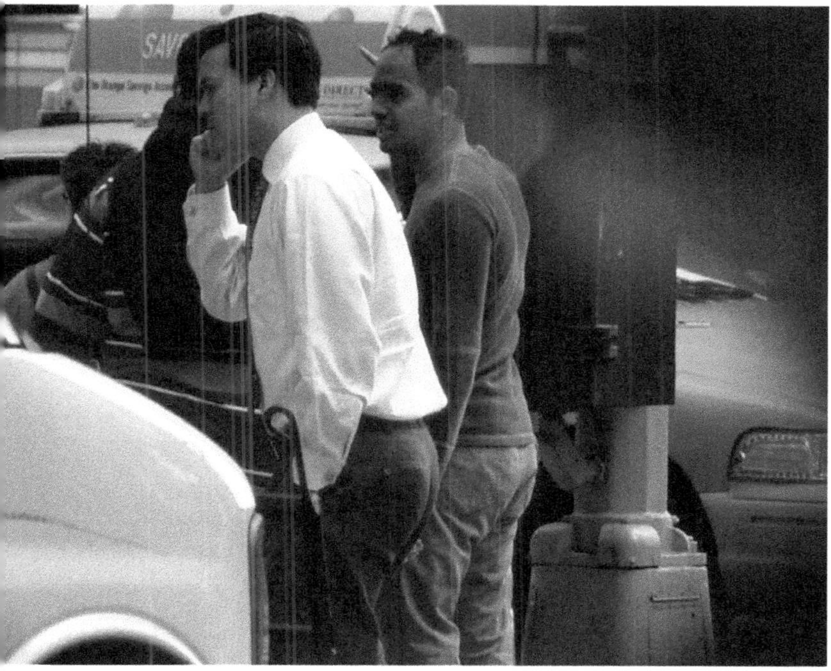

SCHOOL BUS

CHASE

49966-JG

CHILI DOG

PETCO
Where the pets go.

BURGER
BURGER

east midtown
PARTNERSHIP

MYTHSON

FIFTH
ENTRANCE